MW01611766

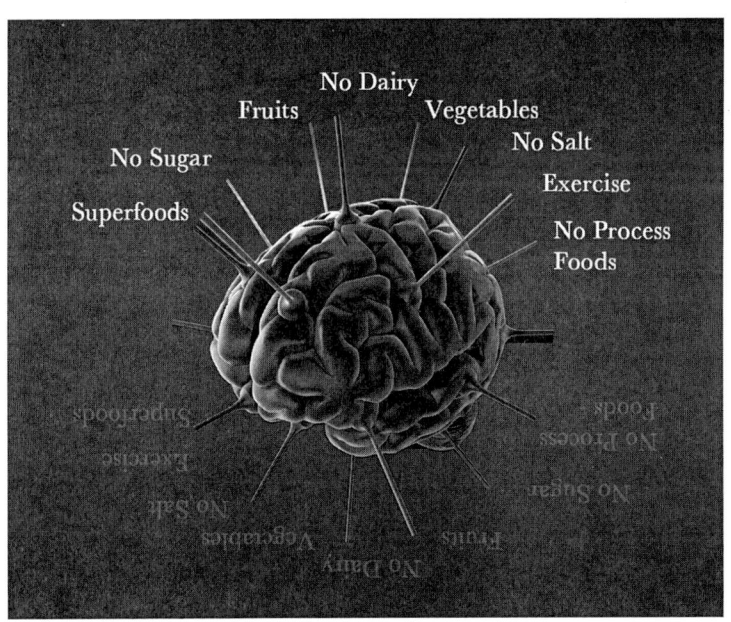

PEACE OF MIND

JAMIE MORGAN BROWN

JAMIE MORGAN BROWN

i ate my way Back to health So Can You!

BY
JAMIE MORGAN BROWN

FOREWORD BY DR. MYLES E. MUNROE

Jamie Morgan Brown
steelpulse2@yahoo.com
www.jmorganbrown.com

Disclaimer:
The author and publisher disclaims all liability associated with this
book. This book is not intended to conflict with any advice given to
you by your physician. If you have a medical condition, please consult your doctor. This material should not be used as a substitute for
any treatment prescribed by your doctor. The information is solely
intended to help you make informed choices about your health.

Cover Photo/Design & Production
Photos, Text Layout and Book Design
reggie rem. erawoc© (erawocbrosgroup®)

Ordering Information/Speaking Engagement
Books can be ordered directly by email; steelpulse2@yahoo.com
or through the website www.jamiemorganbrown.com
Books are available at special quantity discounts when
purchased in bulk by corporations, associations,
libraries, and others, or for colleges.

Library of Congress Cataloging-in-Publication Data
All Rights Reserved.
First Printing, November 2012
Printed in U.S.A.
ISBN 978-0-615-71656-5

I Ate My Way Back To Health / Edited by Jamie M. Brown

To All of Humanity With GOD'S Love

JAMIE MORGAN BROWN

Acknowledgements

I was asked to write this book by so many people after hearing my story. Unfortunately I was not mentally or emotionally stable enough to commit to paper--I just wanted to heal. The mental challenges alone caused me to question God, or even if there was such a power. Boy-o-boy was I humbled. The reality is there's no greater power than God!

Where would we be without our mothers? Mom, thank you for giving me the love that only a mother can provide. You mean the world to me! There was never a moment writing this book when I didn't think about you. I hope your proud of me--it means everything. Having you live with me makes me feel like the luckiest man in the world--I am! To my sister Pam who I love beyond measure. What will it take for you to write published material? You have so much knowledge! Thank you for caring for me. Many days you came and left but I really wished you had stayed. Sharon, I thank you for the help that you provided every single day. The three of you nursed me back to health around-the-clock 24/7 nonstop!

Acknowledgements

I'll never forget those sleepless nights lying in my bed wondering if I was going to recover.
I'll never forget the memories of my head feeling like a brick laying on the pillow waiting for the numbness to go away. Nothing made me happier than waking up every morning knowing that I would see the three of you again.

To my daughter Hanaiya Bahia and my son Kamau, thank you for being the light of my life! The largest nation in the world is the imagination, yet and still, you can't imagine how much you both mean to me. Then again maybe you can! I've come to realize that one of the most important things parents can teach their children is to make good decisions in life. Remember, what you will be you are now in the process of becoming!

To my older brother's Kevin and Bill, I love you both. Let's catch a plane and go to Africa first class my treat! Well, maybe not Africa...and perhaps not first class--and definitely not my treat, but let's go somewhere, anywhere together. Hey Dad your right. Being a father IZ very difficult at times! You deserve more credit than you're given. I can't ever re-

Acknowledgements

member a day hungry, homeless or clothes-less. You provided like a champ and I love you for that. To my main man Reggie Regg, this book would not have been completed without your patience and expertise. You are a good friend, a great father and husband, but slow down. The only thing that never gets tired of running is time. To Erastus Jr. Thank you for writing such an inspirational song, "You Can't See." It's a classic!

To Ahsa Ahla my Godsend, You Are The Truth! You sat in my kitchen and told me if I wanted to live you can show me how--and you did. You didn't ask for a penny! You took my calls when I needed advice, you lifted my spirits when I was down and you made sure I stayed on course. Thank you for inspiring me to get healthy. Friends for life!

Hey Rashaan, forget about the turkey bacon conversations but thank you for checking in and sitting with me. Boy did we laugh! I must give a shout out to your boy Lovell. This brotha told me I was sick months before I even thought about seeing a doctor! Lovell, did I look that bad? It amazes me how some people can see things in you that you can't see in

Acknowledgements
yourself.

Darleen, you are a true friend. You always have been and you always will be. Thank you for the morning visits. By the way you're an awesome mother! Hey Ngaio, thank you for taking me under your wings and showing me the ropes. You're a true mentor!

Barbara, thanx for taking my calls while you was busy at work. You gave me the drive to finish. You believed in me when I had doubts and now I'm done--my very first book!

To all of my Brazilian and Spanish speaking Friends...Com todo o meu coração, Obrigado e Fique com Deus! With all of my heart, thank you and stay with God.

I want to thank my ancestors who gave me the strength, the courage and the will to stand on my square. Most importantly, I want to thank YOU God for keeping me here when you didn't have to. Great decision by the way! I promised you that I would take care of my health for the rest of my life--I won't disappoint-- I promise.

Table of Contents

FOREWORD - Pg.13
DR. MYLES E. MUNROE

AUTHOR'S STATEMENT - Pg.15
JAMIE MORGAN BROWN

P R E F A C E - Pg.19

INTRODUCTION - Pg.23

C H A P T E R S

Chapters Cont.

Foreword

DR. MYLES E. MUNROE
BFM INTERNATIONAL
ITWLA
Nassau-Bahamas

This timely, erudite, eloquent, and immensely thought-provoking work gets to the heart of one of the deepest passions and aspirations of the human heart – good health.

This is indispensable reading for anyone who wants to live a healthy life above the norm. This is a profound authoritative work which spans the wisdom of the ages and yet breaks new ground in its practical approach to regaining and maintaining good health and will possibly become a classic in this and the next generation.

This exceptional work by Jamie Morgan Brown is one of the most profound, practical, principle-centered approaches to the subject of health I have read in a long time.

The author's approach to this timely and critical issue of good health brings a fresh breath of air that captivates the heart, engages the mind and inspires the spirit of the reader to make changes in lifestyles.

The author's ability to leap over complicated scientific and metaphysical jargon and reduce complex theories to simple practical Health principles that the least among us can understand is amazing.

This work will challenge the intellectual while embracing the laymen as it dismantles the mysterious of the soul search of mankind and delivers the profound in simplicity.

Jamie's approach awakens in the reader the untapped inhibiters that retard our desire to discipline ourselves for good excellent health and his personal testimony, antidotes and experience empower us to rise above these self-defeating, self-limiting factors to a life of exploits in spiritual and mental advancement.

The author also integrates into each chapter the time-tested precepts giving each principle a practical application to life making the entire process people-friendly. Every sentence of this book is pregnant with wisdom and I enjoyed the mind-expanding experience of this exciting book. I admonish you to plunge into this ocean of knowledge and watch your life change for the better as you experience the joy of eating your way back to health.

Author's Statement

JAMIE MORGAN BROWN

WESTERN MEDICINE/HOLISTIC HEALING

"When two elephants fight only the grass suffers"
Swahili proverb

Western medicine is the science and practice of treating disease. The conventional approach is through prescription drugs or antibiotics commonly called, The Smart Pill, in alternative social circles. I love western medicine because it saved my life. I love Holistic healing also, because it inspired me to value the life that was saved. It would be a monumental achievement if both respected institutions could find a common ground for the welfare of the people.

The geniuse of both practices are critically valuable and necessary. I do believe there will come a time when medical doctors will look to natural cures for treating sickness and disease. Why not?

When I was diagnosed with cancer I expected my doctor to use the best treatment possible. Being vulnerable and with my life at stake, I wanted to believe the doctor had my best interest at heart. If I'm told I need a new kidney, a heart transplant or chemotherapy, it's because I really need it. I want to trust the decision isn't motivated by greed to buy a yacht or make a substantial lucrative deal. Practicing for profit at the expense of the people is unethical and a great misuse of power!

Since engineers are dedicated to improving technology ... and since scientists are dedicated to improving knowledge in technology and medicine, then, medical doctors must remain dedicated to improving the quality of health of their patients, by learning healthier ways to practice.

Holistic health teaches disease, /dis-ease is a direct result of one's nutritional imbalances which affects the physical, emotional, spiritual, psychological, social and environ-mental imbalances. The holistic approach is treating the symptoms or the cause of the disease while the medical approach primarily treats the disease. Merging both the medical and holistic ideologies, society as a whole would become healthier, smarter and more productive--benefiting all of humanity!

If the United States of America can elect an African American President then all things are possible. America is the richest nation in the free world. There's no reason why she can't become the healthiest nation in the free world as well. When two elephants fight, only the grass suffers.

Preface

JAMIE MORGAN BROWN

*I*t wasn't until I had gotten sick that I realized the importance of eating healthy. Why must something bad always happen before we decide to change? In 2008 I had undergone brain surgery to remove a rare tumor which is found mainly in children. My doctor made it very clear--surgery within ninety days or the possibility of permanent blindness ... or worse!

I experienced blindness, an outer body experience -- and mental torture! I became so depressed I planned my own funeral. Attending Physician, Neurosurgeon Sanjay Gupta MD, along with a team of skilled doctors successfully put me back on the road to recovery. All these experiences caused me to make a change--and I did, forever! A Godsend came to visit me. With clarity he explained to me that if I change the way I eat to a Plant Based Diet, I could live disease-free and enjoy life with optimum health. Needless-to-say, I was sold after that!

The intention of this book is not to lecture you on how to eat or even what to eat. My message to you is simple; your health is your responsibility and the quality of your life, is based on the choices you make in your life.

Hopefully this book will unlock your mind and inspire you to get healthy. It starts with your diet! Regardless of how bad your present health condition is, there's still a chance for you to get better. I'm not going to tell you to stop eating meat. I'm not going to say that an overabundance of meat consumption causes cancer either. I'm neither a licensed doctor nor an authority on nutrition--I'm a survivor! The freedom to eat is one of the only free choices you have in life. You have to find it necessary--for yourself--to want to get healthy. I'm living proof that a plant based diet cures disease. I ate my way back to health, so can you!

This book was not written with medical practitioners, nutritionist or health experts in mind. My purpose is not to challenge any governmental authorities or food lobbyist. This book is for anybody who simply wants to get healthy--but don't know where or how to start. It's for those that either procrastinate, lack the motivation or the will power to make it happen. I want them to know that they can live a healthy, happy, disease free life with nutrition, exercise and lifestyle. This book is for them ... not you!

My victory over the health challenges I endured taught me valuable lessons I wish to share with you. First you must embrace and truly understand your health is your wealth. Without it you have nothing! You are what you eat. Good foods give life and bad foods take it away--that simple. Take good care of your health and your health will take good care of you. Last, and most importantly ... your health is your responsibility!

JAMIE MORGAN BROWN

Introduction
JAMIE MORGAN BROWN

*"The greatest tragedy is not death
but a life without purpose"*
Dr. Myles E. Munroe

During the darkest moment of my life something divine happened. I discovered something I had that I never knew existed before--The Greatness Within! I realized there's something great in all of us. You may not have discovered it yet but its there-- buried inside of you. Throughout all of my travels I have yet to meet anyone who does not possess something great that's extra ordinarily powerful about themselves. As a matter-of-fact I'm convinced we're born with it. Some of us discover our Greatness early in life while other's...*never* find that buried treasure.

In life you'll meet obstacle's that will test your

strength as well as your character. Your greatness will be called upon. You have to know and accept, that You are the champion of your own destiny!

"I Ate My Way Back To Health," is a personal guide intended to inspire and encourage you through your most challenging Obstacles--turning them into Opportunities! My words are documented in two parts. The first part explores the fear of the unknown and accepting the reality that the best way out is through. The second part segues into the solution--health and wellness. Your health is a God given right! Come join me on this journey that will change your life forever.

Chapter One

THE MAILBOX

"What lies behind us and what lies before us are tiny matters to what lies within us."

Ralph Waldo Emerson

Nestled on a pine wood structure that my father and I had built sits a black mailbox. The elongated numbers tipped with a red flag and lazy door gives it an awkward appearance which stands out from our neighbors.

One summer night around ten o'clock I went to get the mail. When I reached my mailbox I stopped to look into the sky. It was a beautiful dark blue sky with a bright white moon--smiling at me. The stars looked like diamonds fixated across the galaxy. I stared at a tiny plane as it silently floated into view and then disappeared into the picturesque background.Everything looked and felt so peaceful and tranquil. There was an eerie midnight calm about this night--I could feel it. As I continued to stare into the stars something quite strange began to happen. Slowly everything started to dim. Right before my eyes the diamond lit navy blue sky suddenly began to fade away. I thought that was quite unusual but I continued to stare. Then my eyes made their way down to the mailbox--my vision was blurred. I knew something was wrong--really wrong! My eyesight was fading. I struggled to see as I placed my hands in front of my face. When I looked into the sky, Bam! ... Lights out! My eyesight disappeared--vanished! Everything went black! I stood still and took a deep breath. I was on the verge of panicking! Nothing I had ever experienced in life prepared me for this moment. I was scared! So scared I couldn't move so I stood there wondering desperately trying not to panic. "I can't see," I said to myself. "God please help me. Please give me my eyesight back please!" I gave it a moment but nothing changed. Now I'm ready to panic! In that very moment my spirit whispered, "Don't panic stay calm." My whole life flashed before me. I kept hearing that voice, "Don't panic stay calm." The thought of me going blind never crossed my mind--but I was! I took a deep breath and somehow

I regained my composure--momentarily anyway.

Moments later in total darkness with my spirit as my guide I took slow tiny steps along my driveway until I reached the garage door. Then, tracing my hands along the banister I felt my way up to the top of my backyard porch. Finally, I made it into the house. In that split second my eyesight reappeared as though someone had turned the circuit breaker back on. I felt a deep sense of relief--boy was I happy! Finally I sat and calmed myself down. I tried to make sense out of what just happened, but nothing -- I drew a complete blank. Something was dangerously wrong and I needed answers, now--Right now! I felt like I was in a bad dream that was about to become ... my worst nightmare.

JAMIE MORGAN BROWN

Chapter Two

MY DOCTOR

"True intelligence is when you can admit you don't know"

When I went to see my doctor I was a nervous wreck. I had a restless feeling about me. The sleepless night before left me in a pensive mood so I was eager to see the doctor. My doctor is thorough and dependable. As far as I was concerned, if there was ever a question regarding my health she had the answer and that's exactly what I needed -- answers!

Although my doctor had been treating me for allergies for over ten years, I just didn't want a routine check up and I certainly didn't want another shot. I needed her to understand there was something seriously wrong with me. I wanted her help, better yet ... I needed it! Not knowing how she was going to respond, I began telling her about what had happened the night before. The story disturbed her. She looked as if she was listening to a narrative from a suspense movie.

Living in Los Angeles, was allergy free for me. I never knew allergies had a season until I moved to Georgia--the pollen capital of the world. I was a sports fanatic who stayed in good shape with a fairly good diet. It all began when I started having trouble breathing, so I went to see a doctor. Initially, I was told that I had asthma. I said, "Asthma, hmm that's strange." Several hours and a few tests later it was confirmed--not asthma, allergies! I went from seasonal allergies and mild headaches to year round allergies and daily headaches. I had a headache every day for ten years--never a day of absence.

After I finished telling her the entire story she seemed bothered. Immediately, she arranged for me to take further tests at a local hospital--so I did. I left her office feeling a bit disappointed because my doctor was clueless about my condition. So far, I was still able to see things in color, however, I knew it was just a matter of time before that terrifying moment would strike again. That was the scary part! I wasn't excited about going to a hospital however that was part of the process. I figured maybe I'll get some answers.

So there I was lying on a hospital bed with all these tubes and wires attached to my body, wondering, "What's really going on!" Hours later another doctor shows up and says, "Mr. Brown you appear to be fine." Other then allergies coupled with a little anxiety your tests look great." Then he suggested that I try a stronger prescription. That irritated me. "A stronger prescription!" I yelled. "That's it!" His non-shallot attitude really bothered me. I felt like tying him up with his own stethoscope. I said, "How in the world--after four hours of testing- nothing could be found! You call yourself a doctor! Perhaps this hospital needs qualified doctor's that know what their doing! Doc, I'm trying to be civil but I'm not leaving here until you all find out what's going on with me!" I yelled. Well I didn't really yell but I wanted to.

I left there confused. I didn't know what to do next, where to go or who to talk to. The only thing I knew was, there was something very wrong with me and I needed help. I felt abandoned. Depression was beginning to set in and socially, I began to slowly drift away. I became a recluse. Never in a million years did I ever think this could happen to me--but it did.

I ATE MY WAY BACK TO HEALTH - SO CAN YOU!

Chapter Three

LIVE EACH DAY TO THE FULLEST

"A danger escaped is no guarantee for the future".
Kikuyu Proverb

Driving my son Kamau to school across town was the start of my day -- 6am sharp! I would warm up the car and sit inside while I waited for him. Usually I would have about a ten to fifteen minute window before he showed up. This particularly cool morning had all the signs of a normal day--at first.

Like most young boys his age, he was eager to drive but not quite old enough yet--only six months left to go. Rarely would a day pass without him asking, "Dad can I drive us to school today? I'll be careful I promise." "Sure you can son," I said, "Soon as you get your permit." My mind was pre-occupied between watching the kids board the school bus and listening to the news on the radio. After the broadcast I turned to another station when disaster struck again--only this time worse! I went blind again, completely--no blur no gray no nothing. I was petrified! I started hyperventilating! It felt like I was having a heart attack. I couldn't breathe. As I struggled for air I could feel my lungs constricting until I finally passed out. This was definitely the end I thought. I just didn't want to die in front of my son.

Moments later, I slowly regained consciousness. Slowly my sight came back again only blurry. Everything looked grey. It was fine with me because I felt lucky at that point. The color gray never looked so beautiful in all my life. Being able to see was more important than seeing in color. I just sat there smiling, happy to see my son heading towards the car. When he finally got in he asked me with a peculiar tone, "Dad are you okay?" "Yes," I said. "I'm fine. Why do you ask?" I was curious because he didn't see what happened--at least I hoped he didn't. I didn't know what was going to happen. On the outside I appeared to be calm but on the inside, I was a nervous wreck. I tried to relax but mentally I felt overwhelmed, exhausted. The idea of confessing crossed my mind but I just couldn't--forget about it.

I prayed for the best and prepared for the

worst, then drove off. About ten minutes into the drive I felt a strange feeling like something was about to happen--and it did. My eye-sight began to fade causing me to drive off the road--just slightly though. My son panicked and grabbed the steering wheel. "Dad what are you doing!" he yelled. I managed to bring the car to a complete stop. "Are you okay?" he asked. "I'm fine, just a little tired that's all, I said." We collected ourselves and drove off slowly. He gave me no indication that he was on to me. My son looks at me as though I'm invincible and this was the perfect moment--not to disappoint him. As far as I was concerned, I was committed to keeping my mouth shut--and that's exactly what I did.

I continued driving. Within a few blocks away from his school, disaster strikes yet again. I couldn't see a thing. This time I drove completely off the road into a ditch. I'm shaken up and so is my son. All I remember was hearing him yell, "Daad!" and in the instant my sight returned. When we arrived at school he got out the car--relieved. "Dad," he asked, "seriously, are you sure your okay? "I'm fine I fine!" I replied. "I told you I'm just a little tired that's all." With an uneasy look on his face he said, "You have me a little worried about you. Make sure you go home and get some sleep."

I took his advice but I didn't wait til I got home. I fell asleep in the school parking lot until lunchtime. After that I woke up and drove all the way home--disaster free.

Chapter Four

THE SUPERMARKET

*"God never promised life would be easy.
He promised it would be worth it"*

On the eve of my son's birthday December 8th 2007 I went to the supermarket to pick up a birthday cake and a birthday card. I was browsing through the card section when I saw my doctor. Occasionally we'd run into each other there and share light hearted conversation. It was the holiday season and the holiday spirit was in the air. After our initial greeting she asked, "Are you still experiencing headaches?" "Interesting you would ask Doc," I replied. "Actually, I have one right now as we're here talking."

By the look on her face she was surprised by my response--I was surprised by her question. She seemed quite perplexed. "Do you still read a lot?" she asked. "Yes, yes I do," I responded. "Why don't you go and get your eyes examined," she suggested. I thought that was ludicrous. The connection between getting my eye's examined and experiencing ten years of daily headaches simply didn't make sense to me. Why hadn't any other doctors suggest an eye exam? I needed answers--not an eye exam. It seemed like a total waste of time and I wasn't up for any more guessing games where I'm the guinea pig. I was getting irritated. I was through talking and ready to go. Inconspicuously, I started looking for the exit door. I felt a sense of disappointment because I wanted my doctor to tell me something definitive, concrete, conclusive--not speculative.

As our conversation was nearing the end she noticed my deep frustration which was quite obvious. She had a contemplative look about her. With piercing eyes she looked at me and said, "Promise yourself that you'll get your eyes examined." I wasn't in the mood to make promises that I had no intention on keeping. I wanted to be honest with her so I told her I would pray on it. She said, "Good that's even better!"

That evening I literally prayed for hours. My spirit whispered, "Hear my servants, they're all around you. The biggest part of the plan of salvation--is faith."

The next morning the first thing I did was to schedule an eye exam. My faith was about to be tested--and it was.

JAMIE MORGAN BROWN

Chapter Five

SUPER BOWL SUNDAY

*"Life isn't about waiting for the storm to pass...
It's about leaning how to dance in the rain"*

Author Unknown

This was the first SuperBowl party that I hosted at my home. I was looking forward to seeing my friends, their guests and having fun. It was Super Bowl Sunday and the joint was jumping! There was plenty of food, music and people everywhere. Everybody was very happy and excited--everybody but me.

As the game got underway I became very concerned. At first everything looked blurry to me but suddenly, without warning the nightmare returned--only this time in front of guests. While everyone was cheering and rooting for their team, once again, my eyesight left me. Seconds later it reappeared allowing me to only see things now in black-n-white. I sat there pretending to act like everything was normal but honestly I was on the edge of going berserk! About five minutes later the color popped back and everything returned to normal--well if you wanna call it that. This was really scaring me. Spoiling the fun for everybody else was not an option so I quietly excused myself and went upstairs to my room.

My bedroom was my sanctuary--a safe haven. I decided to watch the game alone as best I could, however slowly but-surely I was loosing it. Occasionally I would turn away and stare out my window wondering and thinking, thinking and wondering. "God why me?" I asked. "What have I done to deserve this?" I considered myself a man of good character always willing to help others. I was totally confused. All I wanted was to go downstairs, be with my friends and watch the Superbowl. I could hear everybody downstairs rooting and shouting while I was upstairs becoming sadder by the second. Then I heard somebody shout, "Hey where's Jamie!" Wanting not to be disturbed I went downstairs pretending to be fine but I was a ticking time bomb--about to explode.

Inconspicuously, about a half hour later I made it back to my room having survived the spotlight. The more I struggled to watch the game the more frustrated I became. Physically I could literally feel myself dying. Depression became my best friend.

Desperately I tried to watch the game as best I could but it became unbearable, miserable. *Panic took over and I became a madman!*

Filled with rage I grabbed the television and tried to throw it out my window but it wouldn't fit. I yanked all the pictures off the walls, cursing every step of the way. I threw clothes and shoes out my window, books were knocked off shelves, tables turned over--I didn't care anymore. I had enough and I wanted this to be over now--right now!

Finally after about fifteen twenty minutes which felt like an eternity, exhaustion got the best of me. I sat at the edge of my bed and begged for help. "God please help me...pleeease!" I was hoping for a miracle that everything would return to normal but it didn't--and it wasn't. Everything in sight was still colorless. Now I could barely see, I felt like God had abandoned me. The only thing left was to pray--so I did. "Dear God," I began, "this is the scariest moment of my life. Please come into my life and help me. Please grant me the serenity to accept the thing's I cannot change. Give me the strength to change the things I can and the wisdom to know the difference. Protect and bless my family. I love you." After that I went to sleep. By the way...my team won the Super-Bowl.

I ATE MY WAY BACK TO HEALTH - SO CAN YOU!

Chapter Six

A BLESSING IN DISGUISE

"Being defined by honor and redeemed by loyalty is a measure of good character"

Jamie Morgan Brown

A few weeks later I found myself sitting impatiently in the Optometrist office glancing through magazines. I really didn't want to be there to begin with--I really didn't. The thought of leaving crossed my mind several times but each time my spirit whispered, "Stay, don't leave." Keeping good on my promise I made with my doctor did bring a little relief though. I figured this was just a simple routine eye exam done in an hour--well, I figured wrong!

Three hours and several tests later in walks the doctor again for the final time. He had a concerned look on his face. Now I'm nervous! "Is everything okay doctor?" I asked. He pauses, and then he sits down with my chart in his hand. He looks me directly in my eyes and says, " Mr. Brown I have some bad news." My heart dropped. I felt like I was about to faint but I was to afraid. I just took a deep breath and continued to listen. "I found a brain tumor," he says. "It's located directly behind the optic nerve in your right eye. It doesn't look good. I'm going to arrange for you to get a cat scan." He spoke with a clear sense of urgency. "This has to be looked at immediately Mr. Brown," he continued. You can lose your eyesight permanently. You're looking at somewhere around three to six months before you go totally blind." As harsh as it all sounded this was a bittersweet moment for me. On one hand, the thought of going blind was frightening and unimaginable. However on the other hand, I finally found out what was wrong with me. Now I know! The burden had been lifted. This was a bitter victory in itself.

A week later I found myself at the mercy of a Neurologist. He could tell that I was apprehensive about being there even-though he had my full-undivided attention! A few minutes into the exam he says, "Mr. Brown, this is a blessing in disguise. You need to call your doctor and thank her. Had you not gone to get your eyes examined when you did ... and had he not discovered the tumor when he did, you would have either gone blind within the next few months or possibly die in your sleep from a blood clot."

Hearing that almost caused me to loose my mind. The only thing I could think of was how brilliant my doctor was for suggesting that I get an eye exam. "My doctor is brilliant!" I shouted. I bragged about her genius for the remainder of that visit. I'm sure he was glad when I left. For the first time in a long time I felt happy. The spirits of my ancestors were present.

That night I got on my knees and prayed. I realized that it was God who had been whispering to me all along. I asked for his forgiveness. Towards the end of my prayer I said, "Thank you God for being present when I thought you were absent. I love you." For the first time in a long time I went to bed unafraid of closing my eyes.

JAMIE MORGAN BROWN

Chapter Seven

JUDGEMENT DAY

"Wisdom doesn't always come with age but it should come with experience"

African Proverb

Over the next few weeks unfortunately my condition continued to worsen. The mental anguish was breaking me down while the peaks and valleys seemed endless. Even a dog gets tired! I felt like giving up. I knew that I couldn't continue living like this much longer. Ninety days and counting was just around the corner.

One morning I woke up and everything looked gray--for hours. This was the very first time that had ever happened. Usually at the dawn of every morning I see color first. What started as a normal day turned out to be my worst nightmare. It was Judgement day--my life would never be the same again. It all started hours into that afternoon when I realized that I was only seeing in black-n-white--no color whatsoever. This was quite strange because up to this point, I never had a completely colorless day. My concern grew and so did my depression. Trying to keep from panicking I turned on the television--hoping for a miracle. Intuitively, I sensed that my condition was getting worse--and it did. From that day on I never saw color again. My visual reality was black-n-white. I felt alone and trapped in an isolated world. I didn't want to live like this--I was fed up! I decided to change my condition once and for all.

I prayed for a long, long time but even in my silence--I heard no answers. God had turned on deaf ears and for the first time I seriously thought about committing suicide. I became so depressed that I planned my own funeral. After all the funeral arrangements were made I sat in my chair and stared out the window--nature looked so beautiful. I imagined being buried in the richly soiled red earth with green grass blowing above my head--relaxing, chilling and listening to the sound of silence. No more yesterdays, todays or tomorrows--forgetting time and forgiving life--just total peace.

I thought about my family and all my friends. I began to reminisce about all the wonderful moments that God had blessed me with. Then suddenly I began to smile--I found strength again. I had realized that all life is precious. *It was time to drown my fears in the river of courage!*

I ATE MY WAY BACK TO HEALTH - SO CAN YOU!

Chapter Eight

LET GO LET GOD

"Life isn't tied with a bow but it's still a gift"
Regina Brett

When I called to schedule an appointment for the CAT scan the receptionist asked, "Sir, do you have insurance?" Like millions of others I said, "No, no I don't." Then she said, "So you'll be paying out of pocket, cash correct?" " Uh Yes, yes that's correct," I replied. My appointment was scheduled but now there was just one problem. The CAT scan cost almost two thousand dollars ... that I didn't have! I free-lanced in television & film production so being self-insured wasn't an option--I simply couldn't afford health insurance. Just when I thought my problems were solved they were just beginning--and they did.

A few days later I became distraught thinking about finances because I could only afford to pay a fraction of the cost. Shortly after a friend called, a Godsend. Immediately she sensed something was wrong. I told her I was okay but she wasn't buying it. "You don't sound okay" she exclaimed. "I'm coming over, now!" When she arrived we talked for several hours. I explained to her what all I had been going through. I could see that she was deeply saddened--so was I. The very next morning she called and said, "Go get your cat-scan. It's all paid for."--I left so fast you can still see the skid marks in front of my house.

When I arrived at the Image Center, I was a nervous wreck. A couple of hours later two things were confirmed. One, I had a brain tumor and two, surgery was needed asap! Brain surgery is one of the most expensive and complex operations in medicine. To make matters even worse the clock was ticking. Three months total blindness...ninety days was all I kept hearing in my mind. I was facing the frightening reality of either living the rest of my life blind or dying from depression--one or the other. My life was looking bleak. Once again I reached the end of my rope...but I held on tight to prayer. Later that evening, I was in the bathroom praying when some-thing wonderful began to happen.

"Let me make sure I heard you correctly," my spirit whispered. "You've become distraught because you have no insurance, little money and you feel like there's nobody you can turn to for help. Turn to me and look within! This is what I'm going to do for you," it continued. "Listen to me carefully: Not only am I going to provide you with all you need, I'm going to provide the best of all that you need as well. When I'm finished with you, you're going to be healthier than you've ever been in your entire life. Since your tumor is so rare, I'm going to take it all around the world, so doctors can study it and help people all over the earth--my earth! I am the light!"

That night while I was taking a bath I kept hearing the doctor's voice -- "Three months total blindness, ninety day's!" That pressure weighed heavy on my mind--it became unbearable. "Too much pressure busts pipes ... or make diamonds, it whispered." Spontaneously as if someone was listening I jumped up butt naked and shouted, "I'm a diamond!" At that very moment I decided to let go and let God. I guess he has bigger plans for me.

JAMIE MORGAN BROWN

Chapter Nine

MOM

"The greatest love of all"
George Benson

One of the saddest days of my life was telling my mom that I had a brain tumor. The numb look on her face deeply saddened me. It's extremely painful for any parent to watch their child suffer. I went into my room, closed the door and cried for the very first time. Agonizing over this whole ordeal was humiliating for me. Still my fate was yet to be determined. This was a very poignant moment in my life.

Reality hit me after that. If I were to get through this nightmare without having a nervous breakdown, I would have to scrutinize whatever I told mom. My mom is the most loving and beautiful woman in the world, however she has a way of making you feel like you have pneumonia when all you have is a common cold.

My first day in the hospital was like rush hour in a disorganized, overcrowded facility. I was told everything from I might not make it through the night to having a heart attack. Telling mom such depressing information wasn't an option--atleast not on my watch! I had a don't ask don't tell policy which I planned to keep--and I did.

The morning of my biopsy mom wanted to go but I gently told her I wanted to go alone--which was the truth.

The night before I slept uncomfortably--actually I didn't sleep at all. I wrestled with TWI/ The What Ifs. What if it's cancer? What if it's malignant? What if I'm dying? Mentally, emotionally, spiritually and psychologically I needed to face this critical moment with my doctor, alone. Pray for the best prepare for the worst consumed my thoughts all night.

Two weeks later I received the test results and the nightmare was official--cancerous benign, borderline malignant. Now how do I explain that to mom? No longer was I only fighting for my eyesight--now I was fighting for my very life. The doctor suggested radiation treatment immediately. Feeling scared and vulnerable I agreed but my spirit didn't.

All I knew was that I didn't want to die!

When I left the hospital I was deeply depressed, confused and saddened. It all seemed so surrealistic. Over and over again my life flashed before my eyes. The thought of me saying good-bye to all of my love ones was way too much to digest, however this was my reality. Cancer was knocking at my door but I refused to let it in. We both wanted the same thing. In order for cancer to win I must die and in order for me to win cancer must die. I was determined to fight and win--I just didn't quite know how.

I ATE MY WAY BACK TO HEALTH - SO CAN YOU!

Chapter Ten

A GODSEND

*"People come into your life for a reason,
a season or a lifetime"*

African Proverb

The next morning I received a surprise visit from an old friend of over twenty years strong. His presence was like a breath of fresh air. I was happy to see him. Besides him being an accomplished artist, holistic healing and nutrition was his passion. I informed him about the news thinking he would share a few kind words of sympathy--it was just the opposite. The more I spoke the more agitated he became. He continued listening until I finished then he started to speak. He began telling me about food and the importance of eating healthy. Like an enthusiastic student I listened wholeheartedly. His words spoke volume. "You're sick because of the foods you eat," he said. "If you change your diet your diet will change you, "he said. "Cancer cannot live in an alkaline environment. I can help you Jamie if you wanna live." I didn't even know what alkaline meant but I damn sure was gonna find out! Then he smiled at me and said,"I can't cure your cancer but the right foods can." That's all I needed to hear. In my heart I knew I was on the right path to getting healthy. The key to getting healthy is getting started--"Im ready," I said passionately."Whatever he told me to do I did, gladly.

I had never heard anyone connect illness to diet so eloquently and convincingly with words, as he did. "There are herbs that can cure any disease on earth," he continued. Over the next few hours, vehemently he emphasized the importance of me taking responsibility for my own health. "Your health is your responsibility and nobody else's," he preached. That simple statement resonated as I became increasingly empowered by his message.

Then the conversation shifted to the subject about death and dying--which made me a bit uncomfortable. What he asked me next opened my mind like the sun opening a tulip. He asked, "If God sat beside your dying bed and asked, what did you accomplish with the gift of life I gave you? How many people did you help? Who did you serve and whom did you love? What would you say to him Jamie?" Wow! I was speechless--I had no definitive answers. That very moment I realized I had been taking my life for granted as if I was guaranteed another hundred years. I had to make a change. Since change is inevitable it seemed most logical to direct it rather than go through it. If there's to be a future for me it's going to be the result of my diet. Look, you only live once in life and if you do it right...once is enough.

He left later on that evening. I thought about all that he had graciously shared with me. His visit left an indelible impression on me. My future had new meaning. I realized it was my ignorance that made me sick but it's going to be my intelligence that's gets me well.

Throughout that entire evening I prayed. Right before I fell asleep I heard my spirit whisper, "The best way to predict your future is to create it yourself." I chuckled to myself then whispered back, "I know. I'm working on it now." I turned off the light and went to bed. Goodnight.

JAMIE MORGAN BROWN

Chapter Eleven

SURGERY - MY MOMENT OF TRUTH

"Courage is the art of being the only one who knows you're scared to death"

Earl Wilson

The night before surgery I literally prayed myself to sleep--what little I got. That morning I gave my bedroom one last look before leaving. I didn't know if I would ever see my room again--I felt so alone. On our way to the hospital the car was filled with a somber mood void of conversation--just silence the entire ride. To make matters even worse, I lost my eyesight along the way. I chose to remain quiet. As nervous as I was, I was ready. Courage is the art of being the only one who knows you're scared to death.

February 26th 2008, 5am--we arrived at the hospital. Surgery was three hours away and the clock was ticking way to fast for me. I was too nervous to be afraid and too afraid to be nervous. A hospital attendant greeted us. She was friendly and hospitable which had somewhat of a calming effect on me.

A short time later it was time to say goodbye to my family. The nurse gave me a hospital gown then escorted me to the dressing room. "We want to start your IV," she said, "soon as you get dressed Mr. Brown." "Okay," I replied. Then I closed the door.

My mind kept haunting me. It kept drifting back to two defining moments that I just couldn't shake. The first moment happened a few weeks ago during a doctor's visit when an angry looking nurse wheel-chaired me into the x-ray room. The second we got off the elevator she looked at me with a stern look and said, "Once the surgery's done if you live the scar will be very noticeable and unattractive--if. You'll probably have to start wearing hats in public for a long time." At first I thought she was joking but she was dead serious. "I didn't sign up for this!" I exclaimed. I looked up at her and yelled, "Woman what's your problem! Have you lost your damn mind!" Well I didn't quite say it--I wanted to though.

About an hour later I left the hospital, relieved. On the drive home I thought about what that nurse had said which really bothered me. I prayed while I drove all the way home. "Sometimes when people open their mouths," it whispered, "they put their ignorance on display. Two things are infinite, the universe and human stupidity." I just couldn't believe that anyone could be so insensitive, especially at a time like this. My spirit inspired me to shine brighter than her darkness. I had to forgive that lady because I understood ... "Hurt people, hurt people."

The second defining moment was when a conservatively dressed administrator called me into her office to sign papers. "Close the door and have a seat," she said. Nervously I did. Her demeanor felt welcoming at first so politely I asked her, "Ma'am can you please explain to me exactly what am I signing?" "Sure Mr. Brown," she responded, "These papers indicate in case you die or if anything goes wrong during surgery the hospital won't be held liable. If you die it won't matter to you anyway." "Oh boy here we go again. This must be some sort of prank," I said to myself. If it was it wasn't funny! I was so nervous after that, the thought of not having surgery sounded like a great idea. When I left her office I went inside the bathroom and prayed. Then I prayed again, and again. "Be strong. I'm with you," my spirit whispered. "God does not allow anything to interfere with his power and authority." I struggled to get my mind prepared for what was about to happen.

Finally it was the moment of truth. Time to say goodbye. With my family surrounding me the Anesthesiologist smiled and asked me to count to ten. The last number I remembered was...four. Light's out! Now I'm in Gods hands.

Chapter Twelve

THE AWAKENING

*"Three things cannot be hidden
the sun, the moon, and the truth"*

Buddha

*H*e transported me through this eerie dimly lit cave-like tunnel which had a strange and mysterious feel to it. It was cold and creepy! I had no clue where I was or where I was going. Later I found out that it was the hospital basement. Feeling chills running through my body, in a groggy voice I asked, "Am I going to surgery now?" He looked at me and gently said, "Surgery is over. I'm taking you to your room, just relax." All of a sudden that dimly lit cave-like tunnel didn't feel so strange or mysterious after all--and the temperature was just fine.

The doctor came to my room and asked me how was I feeling? I told him I felt great! "Fine," I said. "I feel so good Doc I can't believe I had brain surgery this morning." He looked at me and started laughing. "What are you laughing at?" I asked. He said, "Mr. Brown you just woke up after over thirty hours of sleep. You slept almost a day-n-a-half. I'm just here to let you know your surgery went very well."

It seemed like only a few hours ago when I was counting to ten. About an hour later another doctor came to my room. He was very inquisitive. I told him about the dream I had--he listened closely. I dreamt that I had awakened and stepped out of my body. Relaxed, I turned around and stared at myself sleeping. I looked so peaceful--so comfortable. The eyes caught my attention immediately! They re-minded me of how a persons eyes look when they're laying in a casket. The thought that I may have tran-sitioned never entered my mind, not once. I felt loved. I felt welcomed--I felt at home. Wherever it was, I knew I was in a very special place--in a very special time.

I stood at the corner of the bed and saw two beautiful bright lights, one white and the other a beautiful sky blue. As I walked toward the bright lights I came upon a window without glass, castle-like. I stood there overlooking the beautiful blue green ocean waves and the turquoise blue sky. It seemed as though I could've reached out and touched the cotton white clouds as they floated by. Everything felt so perfect, so tranquil--so visceral. It felt like what I imagined heaven to feel like--perhaps it was. My spirit led me to walk back toward my bed. I stopped and stared at myself one last time. Then I turned around and slowly laid back into my body.

Honestly, I didn't expect the doctor to believe my story but he did. He told me I had an out of body experience. "Get some rest Mr. Brown," he said. Then he left.

If you tell me a fact I'll remember it. If you tell me you love me I'll feel it. However, if you tell me a good story--I'll remember it forever!

JAMIE MORGAN BROWN

Chapter Thirteen

THE POWER OF PRAYER

"Prayer is perfect communication with God"
Jamie Morgan Brown

Prayer is God breathing into us. It's our first obligation to him. Prayer is our highest calling and our most intimate and honest expression of our thoughts and wishes.

My second Godsend was the first person to visit me when I got home from the hospital. She told me something powerful had happened during my surgery. "Oh really. What happened?" I asked. She began telling me about a Global Prayer she organized with some of her friends...whom I've never met before. "We prayed for you Jamie," she said tearfully. "At 8 o'clock that morning friends from Atlanta, California, New York, Jersey, Brazil, Canada and Africa all prayed at the same time. We prayed for your surgery to go well and be a success." I didn't know how to respond to her after hearing that. My emotions got the best of me. I spoke silently--I was speechless. This was the most humbling moment I had ever experienced in my life. My heart was filled with joy. I just sat there, overwhelmed.

That night, feeling elated I began to write--If all the sky was paper and all the trees were pencils, there still wouldn't be enough space to express my deepest gratitude to all those who prayed for me. Her story left an indelible imprint in my heart. It's true--when prayers go up blessings do come down. *Amen.*

Chapter Fourteen

THE WAR OF THE GOD'S

*"In the land of the blind the man
with one eye is still king"*

Ancient Kemit

*P*ost surgery, my first visit to my new doctor wasn't what I expected. He seemed irritated when I told him that I wasn't taking any more medication since finishing the prescription. Changing to a plant based diet became a way of life for me, plus--I felt great. This didn't sit to well with the doctor though. With a stern voice he said, "Mr. Brown you must continue to take your medication! You still need radiation treatment." I wanted to ask him why but something inside me said just listen--so respectfully I did. Radiation treatment was the furthest thing from my mind. I had read countless accounts of people curing cancer through nutrition. Besides, it just felt like the natural thing for me to do.

He seemed irritated then called my surgeon. "Hello doctor," he said, "Are you aware that Mr. Jamie Brown stopped taking his medication?" Seconds later he handed me the phone and then the doctor asked me a series of questions. I told him that over-all I was feeling fine. He reiterated the success of my surgery and then parted with words of encouragement. Moments later the doctor started talking to me about tumors. I asked, "What causes tumors doctor?" "That's the million dollar question." he replied. "Medical research believes people are either born with tumors or they develop at an early stage. Life's experiences triggers them to mutate.

He explained to me that my tumor is mainly found in infants and children...up to around age eleven. I thought that was interesting. Then he said, "We're interested in studying your tumor for medical research Mr. Brown. There's very little data on anyone your age living with such a tumor. Post brain surgery requires that medication be taken for a minimum of one year--no exceptions. You stopped taking all medication after only ninety days. Plus Mr. Brown," he said, "You don't look like a person who had brain surgery just three months ago. Of course we're all happy about the outcome, however we did have concerns about your vision. We didn't know if you would be able to see so soon, at least three to six months. We were prepared to stitch your eyes shut so you couldn't put pressure on the nerve. Your tumor was the size of two golf balls pre-surgery. When we went inside it shrunk-to under half that size. How that happened or why there's no definite explanation," he said. I was certain my diet played a huge role in my recovery. Since surgery was inevitable I was determined to do whatever I could to help myself--and that I did. I became a Vegan. The doctor continued by saying, "Seizures are common after brain surgery yet you haven't had any." Hearing all this made me nervous. I didn't know if I was supposed to be happy or sad--but I certainly started to feel paranoid.

"What are you doing Mr. Brown to look so healthy," he asked? I told him I changed the way I eat to a plant based diet. "You still need medication!" aggressively he exclaimed. "I strongly suggest you start radiation treatment as soon as possible." He totally dismissed everything I told him as if my diet couldn't have contributed at all. That really annoyed me! He continued to talk I continued to listen--actually I tuned him out. My attention flashed-back to that moment in the bathroom when I was praying. "Not only am I going to provide all that you need, I'm going to provide the best of what you need. When I'm finished with you," it whispered, "you're going to be healthier than you've ever been in your life"--I am. I kept hearing those words over and over again. Today my tumor is being studied and helping people all around the world; Puerto Rico, Cuba, Africa and India.

Nature teaches us that there's a cure for every disease right in the earth. Question-Who's in charge of the earth? You're right the Most High. I'd rather trust God's ignorance than man's highest intelligence.

Chapter Fifteen

PATIENCE IS A VIRTUE

"Love the life you live...
live the life you love"

Midnite

*T*hat dreadful morning I wanted to avoid finally arrived. It was time for my first radiation treatment at the cancer center. Mentally I was so not ready for this. I was greeted by the staff and then taken to a room to undress and get prepared. I just couldn't understand why I needed radiation at this point. My diet was excellent, my eyesight was improving, no headaches, no seizures--no nothing! I was getting healthier by the day, every day.

Being at the center was depressing. I just wanted to go home. About fifteen or so minutes later, in walks a doctor. "Good morning Mr. Brown," he begins. "We're just moments away now. Make yourself comfortable. I'll be back shortly." When he left I wanted to lock the door behind him but I didn't-- I really really wanted to, I really did. I kept thinking about my friend who lost her mother due to chemotherapy treatment. She told me the story about the bond between her seventy five year old mother and her older twin sister. "They were inseparable," she said. "My mom and her sister did everything together from laundry to shopping plus everything else in between. Often-times they were accused of neglecting the rest of the family just to spend time amongst themselves."

One day her mom complained about having chest pains. Immediately she called her sister and off to the doctor they went. About an hour and several tests later they were both diagnosed with having cancer. Her family was devastated! She explained to me that her family has a history of cancer which was passed down over the generations. Anyway, the doctor urgently suggested chemotherapy treatment immediately--so they started. The older sister didn't like the after effects from the treatments so she decided to stop. Someone suggested looking into alternative approaches, so she did. She began looking for natural cures for cancer on the internet. Within minutes she found several cures at her fingertips. She began treating it--naturally. Filled with mixed emotions, immediately she called her twin sister but she wasn't interested in stopping her treatments. Like the rest of her family she begged her older sister to continue getting chemotherapy. The family tried repeatedly to persuade her to change her mind. They accepted and believed that cancer runs in the family and chemotherapy is the cure. The older twin still refused. She was determined to stay the course--the natural way. Hearing all this triggered me back to quoted medical information I came across sometime ago. "Cancer treatment is defined as surviving surgery chemotherapy and radiation for five years. If you die of cancer in the sixth year the treatment is still considered a success."

Anyway, let's get back to my story. Six months later after cleansing and changing completely to a plant based diet her cancer totally disappeared, gone! Her family rejoiced and celebrated her recovery. Unfortunately her mom continued her treatment and passed away seven months later.

Her story haunted me while I waited for the doctor to return. An hour went by, then another, still no doctor. Finally, after waiting four grueling hours the door opens. In walks my doctor along with two others. My nerves were about to explode! "Which one of these doctors is going to break the bad news?" I wondered. For a moment I thought about running out of the room but the possibility of being grabbed then put in a straight jacket and thrown in a psycho ward scratched that idea. For some strange reason I thought about the movie, "One Flew Over The Coo koo's Nest." My mind wasn't clear at all--I was in a state of trepidation! I could see the doctors mouth moving but I didn't hear anything. I took a deep breath and braced myself. After what seemed like an eternity the doctor finally says, "Mr. Brown sorry for taking so long but I have some news for you. I interrupted. "How long do I have to live doc?" I rudely blurted out. The room grew silent. Then he continued, "We got together and took another look at your lab results. We conferenced for quite sometime." It seemed as though he was trying to find a subtle way to tell me I was going to die. I said, "Please just give it to me straight. How much longer do I have to live, just tell me?" In silence they stared at each-other which was pissing me off!

Then what he said next totally blew me away. "Mr. Brown," he begins, "Yes you are going to die however just not today. We couldn't find a trace of cancer anywhere in your body--it disappeared. No radiation treatment needed. You can go home."

That was the last thing I heard the doctor say. Before he finished his next sentence I was already home--smiling from ear-to-ear.

I ATE MY WAY BACK TO HEALTH - SO CAN YOU!

Chapter Sixteen

THE ADDRESS

"Peace is costly but it's worth the expense"

An Ivorian Proverb

Clueless about how my medical bills were going to be paid I was determined to leave a zero balance, somehow someway. At first this whole ordeal from the very beginning up to now seemed like a major set-back in my life. Then I realized that a set-back is really a set-up for a comeback! I just knew that there was so much more I wanted and needed to accomplish in my life. I was thankful to be alive.

Wearing a happy face and enjoying every breath of my new life I arrived at the hospitals business office. A clerk was typing behind her desk. Eagerly I said to her ,"I'm here to make a payment." She was very courteous. "Can I please have your name and social, "she asked? "Gladly," I replied. I had a one hundred dollar bill in my pocket and I couldn't wait to make my first payment. Seconds later she looked up at me and said, "Jamie Brown?" "Yes that's me," I responded. "Sir your bill was paid already," she said. "Are you sure?" I asked. "Yes. Your bill was paid a few weeks ago," she said. After I picked my face up off the floor I asked her, "Ah Ma'am, does it say who paid it by any chance?" "No sir it doesn't," confidently she replied. You need to thank whoever it was that's for sure." I agreed then thanked her as I walked away. I was totally dumbfounded, bewildered. Days passed as I exhausted myself wondering...who paid my bill?

A few weeks later it was time for my next appointment. I figured now is the perfect time to satisfy my curiosity. I was anxious to ask the doctor about my bill. My best guess was that the hospital paid for it since my tumor was being used for medical research. After a few hours of running tests it was time to leave, but not without answers. This was the moment for resolve--I went for it. He smiled and politely said, "No Mr. Brown the hospital didn't pay your bill. Perhaps it was someone who loves you dearly." "Doc," I said. "That's a hell-of-a lot of love. Who could possibly love me that much?"

I paused for a moment. "Could it have been a

philanthropist maybe?" I asked. "No Mr. Brown it was not a philanthropist. Why are you so concerned about who paid the bill? Just be thankful that it was paid," he said. "Doc," I declared, "You don't understand! Knowing who paid my bill is extremely important to me." Then he asked me, "Why is it so important to you?" I told him that I was very curious. "I want to thank whoever it was and send them a gift," I said. All I ask and all I need is a simple name and address doc that's all." He paused then asked, "What if I told you God paid it then what?" "Then that's great!" I said excitedly. "Now all I need is God's address." The room went silent for a moment. Then he asked me an unambiguous question. "Mr. Brown are you a praying man?" "Yes, yes I am doctor," I replied. "I am a praying man but why do you ask?" He stopped what he was doing then looked at me. With a smile on his face he said, "Well then you already have God's address."

Chapter Seventeen

MY LIFE

"Man Guesses but God knows"
Jamie Morgan Brown

"*M*y life is dedicated to getting healthy and helping as many people as I can along the way!" The doctor told me the tumor would return in three to four years, malignant...I would not live.

How long I live will not be decided by a doctor,
it will be decided by God.

As you slowly TURN to the next few pages,
you will see my response to that doctor's prediction!

JAMIE MORGAN BROWN

Chapter Eighteen

LEARN HOW TO TAKE CARE OF YOURSELF

"If you don't understand the importance of food or how it nourishes the body, then, what you think you understand will only confuse you!"

Jamie Morgan Brown

When it comes to our health many of us simply don't know how to take care of ourselves. Where to begin or how to begin seems like an arduous process but it's really not--truthfully it's quite simple. As long as we can function most of us believe our health is good. Unfortunately just because you're not sick doesn't mean you're healthy. Usually it's not until we have what I call a Scared Straight Moment, before we start paying attention to our health. It's the dawn of a new day my friend so we must begin to familiarize ourselves with our bodies and our health.

While we pay attention to the need for protein--with the help of television advertisements-- not enough is said about the importance of minerals. Far to often we are programmed with information that doesn't work in our best interest. The most valuable resource you can pay to someone--is your attention! We must question the motives and agendas of those we want to trust.

Minerals help regulate body functions and build the structures in the body like teeth and bones. Your body is an electrical machine that runs off of electricity. Minerals help send electrical frequencies throughout the body. It houses electrical forces that nature provides to maintain itself. Your computer needs an electrical charge to work--correct? Well your body needs an electrical charge in order to work also. You cannot live without minerals because your cells depend on them.

Take the initiative to find out what herbs and minerals are best for you. We seem to get sick when we can least afford or least expect to--sometimes both. We place our health in the hands of our doctors instead of ourselves! Sometimes it's necessary, other times it's not. As a result we've become chemically dependent on antibiotics. You are your best doctor. Nobody knows you better than you! Not taking re-sponsibility for your health is what made you sick.

It's time to reverse the process so that you can get well.

Learn how to take care of yourself. Familiarize yourself with herbs & minerals. Herbs, referred to as natural medication is another name for natural food or God's food. The main purpose of food is to give life! Sustain it by eating foods that will maintain the body on a cellular level. The cells must be nourished with nutrition. Herbs cleanse, sanitize and build the body which energizes the body so that it can heal itself.

The first step to good health is to Cleanse/Fast. This helps to create balance and revitalizes the cells in the body. Start with your colon! Cleansing is extremely important to restoring and maintaining good health. It purifies your mental, physical and spiritual well-being. The next simple step is learning what to eat and what not to eat. Go back to nature! The best foods for your body are found in the earth. Not only is optimum health a human right, it's a God given right. Your health is your responsibility!

Helpful Tips To Health: When you're hungry eat healthy...
1. Avoid Snacking, 2. Exercise at Least 3 to 4 Times a Week,
3. Drink Water, 4. Rest and get enough Sleep,
5. Keep a Positive Outlook on Life, and
6. Never Stop Believing in Yourself!

JAMIE MORGAN BROWN

Chapter Nineteen

HEREDITARY / GENETICS

"Leadership is the capacity to influence others through inspiration motivated by passion, generated by vision, produced by conviction, ignited by purpose"

Dr. Myles Munroe

Remember my friend who lost her mom due to cancer? Well after hearing me talk about how I cured my cancer she asked if I could help her. "Of course," I said. "It's all about your diet." She was very receptive when I explained that cancer cannot live in an alkaline body. I told her she would have to change to a plant based diet. She agreed so we began.

When I asked her about her mother's twin sister that brought a smile to her face. "My favorite auntie is doing fine!"she rejoiced. "Auntie's my inspiration." She told me that as far back as she could remember her family had a history of cancer for generations. "It's hereditary, genetic," she concluded.

I disagreed with her. I explained to her that physical characteristics like the eyes, ears, nose and lips are results of genetics, hereditary. Cancer, diabetes and high blood are the results of a poor diet. She told me that poor diets ran in her family for generations. "And that's why for generations your family has a history of cancer," I said. "You all ate the same food sources. Change the food in the family and the condition of the family will change as well."

She was resolute about eliminating cancer from her family once-and-for all. She took charge and became a leader. With an unbridled focus she began to take the necessary steps--she did the work. Through cleansing and improving her diet her health improved drastically.

"What about my family?" she then asked. There were concerns about being met with resistance--she was. Wholeheartedly she knew that persuading her family to eat healthier would be a colossal task. Her favorite, uncle Larry didn't hesitate to voice his opinion. "I'm not changing a damn thing!" he vented. "Especially not my pork, chitlins or fried chicken! Grandmom and Grandad ate like this for years and so am I." For a long time her family shared those convictions until a year later when Uncle Larry suffered a massive heart attack. He passed away four months later from heart disease.

Slowly but-surely, one-by-one her family began to embrace her new philosophy--Health First! She understood that accepting a genetically predisposed disease excused her of the responsibility of finding a cure. The day when cancer will permanently be eliminated from her family echoes in her daily prayers. Dreams of a healthy future shine bright for her children now, and their children, and their children's children--for generations to come.

JAMIE MORGAN BROWN

Chapter Twenty

KNOWLEDGE IS POWER

"My people are destroyed for lack of knowledge"

The Most High

Most Americans eat the same basic foods; meat, rice and bread that contains dairy, salt and sugar. What's interesting to me is that People Of Color suffer disproportionately without a clear understanding as to Why? According to statistics People of Color have the poorest health then any other race of people in America. My curiosity and research led me to researching the molecule called Melanin. My findings led me to some amazing discoveries!

What is Melanin? Melanin is a molecule that's produced in the pineal gland. It is mostly associated with skin pigmentation however, the benefits of melanin are endless. Melanin regulates all mental and physical body functions. Every organism on earth contains Melanin--even your food! For People Of Color Melanin **recycles** food, good or bad that's digested in the body. This means it delivers a double-dose of the toxins and chemicals which eventually breaks down your health. It is vital for People Of Color to eat nutritionally. Perhaps this is what Dr. Llaila Afrika, world renowned nutritional consultant and historian was referring to when he said, "When we get sick we get twice as sick!"

Ahsa Ahla, one of the leading authorities on nutrition explains it this way. "People of Color suffer with chronic and degenerative diseases more then any other race. This is due to an over abundance of acid in the body that's not producing enough alkaline, causing disease. The body is made up of cells. Acid destroys cells and Alkaline keeps them healthy. This is why it's important to eat foods that have nutritional value." He concluded by saying, "We have to realize we are Melanin dominate people and our foods must reflect that."

Another noted scholar on the subject, Preventive and Holistic Physician Dr. Jewel Pookrum, M.D, states, "Melanin plays an important role regarding health. High concentrations of protein and animal fat are not good for People Of Color. There has to be a need for us to know ourselves and come into an understanding of who we are."Another authority on the subject writes, "Melanin is the hardest molecule to ever be analyzed. It is highly resistant to digestion by most acids. If you don't purify your melanin molecule you will not heal your body of diseases," he concluded.

People Of Color have documented works on Melanin that is extremely vital for you to familiarize yourself with. I wonder why this topic remains omitted from the mainstream?

I understand why children are afraid of the dark...I just don't understand why adults are afraid of the light.

Chapter Twenty - One

MAKE BETTER CHOICES

"You are the sum total of your choices"

Dr. Wayne Dyer

It's easy to make unhealthy food choices living in such a fast paced high demanding environment where time becomes an issue and rushing becomes the catalyst for emotional eaters. For many of us it's even easier to make unhealthy choices when it's decided by economics. We lose our health to make money and then we lose our money to restore our health. This can send you on an emotional roller coaster. When it comes to making decisions emotions can get in the way.

Sometime ago, I heard a lecture by a world-renowned doctor that really moved me. He talked about health and longevity and how emotions are associated with our eating habits. I've witnessed doctors and scholars take the podium on the subject but this particular lecture hit home. I saw myself in those words--it really broadened my perspective. He spoke about how salty foods redirects anger, frustration and violence and how crunchy foods help release anxiety and pressure. He commented on creamy foods helping to satisfy the need to be nurtured and comforted. Then he started talking about chewy foods. "Chewy foods," he said, "relieves tension and promotes the need to slow down and unwind." His statements really resonated with the audience as the lecture was coming to a close. "Bready foods," he said, "relieves feelings of insecurity and soothes dissatisfaction. Sugar, the biggest drug in the world, helps satisfy the need to give and receive love." I was really inspired by that lecture.

Making better food choices using your intelligence rather than emotions will not only promote a healthier lifestyle, it will also bring balance to your life.

*Suggestion:
Add fresh fruits, vegetables and whole grains to your diet.
You'll feel better, sleep better and have more energy.

Chapter Twenty - Two

KEEP IT SIMPLE KEEP IT REAL

"In the abundance of water the fool is thirsty"

Bob Marley

One Sunday afternoon on a seven hour drive home from Florida the four of us shared stories about the fun-filled weekend we had salsa dancing in Orlando. A couple of stories later I found myself fully immersed in a discussion about health and wellness. This particular story grabbed my attention. It was so powerful yet so simple that I felt the need to write about it with her permission. She's Russian. Her story began by telling me that a few years ago she experienced difficulty breathing. At first she thought it wasn't anything major but it had worsened over the next few days--her concerns grew. She decided to go to the doctor for help. Being healthy was very important to her and believing in her doctor was equally as important.

Hours later after all the exams and tests were completed she was told she had asthma. A medicated inhaler was the doctor's recommendation. Not only were the doctor's findings disturbing, her intuitions told her it had to be a misdiagnosis. She decided to get a second opinion only this time she flew back home, to see 'her doctor. After being questioned and completing the consultation process her doctor said, "You don't have asthma at all. Since your diet is pretty good I recommend you include running and swimming to your lifestyle a few times a week." Happy hearing the news she flew back to america following her doctor's advice. Today her breathing is back to normal and she hasn't experienced any abnormalities ever since. Oftentimes what's really needed is information and not medication.

The sad part is children and adults living with asthma are told to refrain from running or being excessively active. Diet as a cure...is seldomly mentioned.

Her experience reminded me of a 'good story I heard a doctor tell about George Washington the first president of the United States. The simplicity and the message of this story make it so compelling to me. It goes something like this: George Washington had a raging fever. He was bed ridden with seven doctors standing around his bed. The doctors refused him water thinking it would worsen his condition. Moments later he died and one of the doctors said, "Maybe we should've given him water." End of story.

Man, with all his brilliance can easily be defeated by his own ego. "A wise man never knows all, only fools know everything." *African Proverb.*

JAMIE MORGAN BROWN

Chapter Twenty-Three

DIET

*"Just because you like the smell of a rose
beware of its thorns"*

Author Unknown

One of the main reasons why people diet is to lose weight, which is usually the process. Enthusiastically you start the diet and lose a few pounds then celebrate, modestly. Slowly the weight returns like a bad dream. Time passes then a new diet is introduced and off to the races you go, again...only to experience the same disappointing results. After talking with people over time I'm convinced diets do not work. In my opinion, the reason is because your emphasis is misplaced. Instead of you focusing on losing weight, perhaps the focus should be on getting healthy! After all isn't that the ultimate goal? Let's understand something, the only person who benefits from the diet is the person who created it. The reality is, when your mindset is on getting healthy, weight loss becomes inevitable at that point. Question- What's the sense of losing weight if you're still unhealthy? Losing weight doesn't make you healthy, eating healthy makes you healthy--plus lose weight.

One morning while I was sitting in the Jacuzzi at the gym I overheard two friends talking about losing weight. The term 'diet was being tossed around like a salad. He expressed his frustrations about dieting and then told her he really needed help. He said he'd tried countless diets for years and at age forty-two nothing seemed to work. She encouraged him to try a new diet which had worked for her, at first. Jokingly he said, "I don't want to make a good looking corpse at such a young age." They laughed. I wanted to butt in but my spirit guided me to just listen--I was the fly on the wall.

A few weeks had passed before I saw him again only this time I took the initiative. Politely I introduced myself and then asked him about his diet. "Miserable!" he exclaimed. "I'm so frustrated trying to lose this weight I don't know what to do!" I asked if I could make a suggestion. "Sure," he replied, "Why not?" My suggestion was that he totally forget the idea of losing weight. Instead, plant the seed of getting healthy in his mind. He stared at me and then smiled as if a light bulb had been turned on. We talked for over two hours that day. We were both happy when we parted.

A year later and seventy pounds lighter sporting his new swagger, he recognized me at a sporting event. He-looked-great! Excitedly he couldn't stop talking about how great he felt and how wonderful life has become--all because of his health. I missed half that game listening to him talk about how his life has changed for the better. I didn't mind...well maybe just a little. I asked about his female friend who had encouraged him about trying her diet some time ago. He said they spoke recently over the phone for the first time in months--the table had turned. She expressed her frustrations about dieting. "I really need help," she said. "I don't want to make a good looking corpse at such a young age neither!" She cried out for his help so the very next day they met. She was blown away by how good he looked. The rest was history.

I ATE MY WAY BACK TO HEALTH - SO CAN YOU!

Chapter Twenty - Four

AN I-OPENER

"Not to know is bad. Not to wish to know is worse."

African Proverb

*I*t happened on a Saturday afternoon. My eighty year old mom and I went to the health food store to do our bi-weekly shopping. She mentioned that she had an urge for something sweet so she decided to buy a slice of cake. Within one minute we found ourselves planted in the bakery section. The wide range of assortments looked so delicious that my mother's sweet tooth started growing fangs. A few cookies was added to the chart. I told her that the ingredients included natural sweeteners instead of sugar -- so I thought. I figured since we're in a health food store the food would be healthy, right? Wrong, dead wrong! After reading the ingredients we realized that white sugar was added. I asked an employee to explain why would a health food store use white sugar instead of natural ingredients. Customer friendly, she informed us that every sweet item in the store contained either sugar, dairy or animal products. She said, "All health food stores do." Hearing that really bothered me--I felt manipulated. In my naivety I wanted to honestly believe health food stores sold health food products, period. Reality set in. The health food industry is a business like any other business and the main objective in business is profit -- sad but true.

This puts the responsibility of your health in your hands and nobody else's. Before you buy anything edible at any store, make sure you read the ingredients first! Your body is the garden and you are the gardener. Fill your garden with foods that will nourish you with optimum health.

Remember, health reform will never be found in any government, store or restaurant. True health reform can only be found in one place and one place only--in your own kitchen!

Chapter Twenty - Five

BREAKING OLD HABITS
CAN SAVE YOUR LIFE

*"Do the best you can until you know better.
Then when you know better, do better."*

Maya Angelou

When it comes to eating, meat is probably the most consumed dietary practice today. When asked why meat, the most common answer is protein. Question? Why eat the animal for the protein when you can get the protein first hand from the same source the animal got it from? Think about it. Did you know your body produces protein naturally? Yes, the body needs protein...but how much?

Remember the famous phrase, Got Milk? Most people drink milk for the calcium. They say it's good for the bones. If that's true then why do statistics show countries consuming the highest amount of dairy have the highest amount of osteoporosis-disease of bones? According to food and health experts, Dairy is Mother Nature's perfect food. It is if you're a calf. Human beings are the only ones that drink milk from other animals. Cows get their calcium from plants that are rich in magnesium because according to experts, their milk has insufficient magnesium content. Calcium is found in every natural plant and sea vegetation. Grains like Quinoa, Teff and Amaranth are all high in calcium. What about the Super Food Chia Seeds? Did you know chia seeds offer six times more calcium than whole milk, three times more iron than spinach and fifteen times more magnesium than broccoli?

Mark Hyman M.D, along with other practicing physicians link dairy to Prostate cancer. "Dairy is full of saturated fats," he says, "which can lead to heart disorders. It can cause digestive problems, allergies, sinuses, ear infections, type 1 diabetes, constipation and anemia in children as well."

What about salt? It too must be eliminated. Too much salt can be deadly. It leads to water retention which leads to weight gain. Consequently this adds pressure to the heart to pump blood throughout the body. Salt also leads to high blood pressure which leads to a list of other medical diseases. A much healthier supplement is Sea Salt. Unrefined sea salt contains a lot of important minerals that regular iodized salt does not. White sugar must be eliminated without question. It is not food. It's a drug and all drugs are addictive! It contains no vitamins, minerals nor fiber whatsoever. Even though sugar taste good it causes a mountain of problems like headaches, depression, hypertension, obesity, heart disease, violence, kidney and colon damage just to name a few. Sugar decays the immune system's ability to protect the body leaving it vulnerable to fight against infections. Since it causes tooth decay knowing that teeth are the hardest part of the body, imagine the damage it's doing to the rest of your organs. There are alternative natural sweeteners like Stevia, Raw Honey, Agave nectar and Fructose in its natural form.

Today, being sick or unhealthy is your choice. When the doctor informs you of a medical problem your responsibility is to find natural and holistic treatments. I'm not suggesting stop seeking medical attention because medical doctors are necessary. They help save lives. However, while the doctor is helping you...you can help yourself. Get Right or get Left!

I ATE MY WAY BACK TO HEALTH - SO CAN YOU!

Chapter Twenty - Six

I'M TALKING ABOUT A MAN IN THE MIRROR

"The path is made by walking."

African Proverb

People living with a deadly disease showing no sense of urgency to cure it puzzles me. A student of mine told me he had been living with diabetes for years and it had taken a toll on his body. Mentally and emotionally he was committed to training however physically, he wasn't able to. He was on dialysis which seemed to bother me more then him. "It's just a matter of routine," he said, "I'll be okay." I felt a sense of responsibly because I knew I could help him. It amazes me how people can look so healthy yet be so sick. Anyway we talked that night over the phone and agreed to meet the next day, we did. He was in good spirits when we met and so was I. We talked for a while. I suggested he watch a CD about curing diabetes by adopting a Plant Based Diet. He was very thankful for my generosity and promised to watch it that evening. "This was going to be a no-brainer," I said to myself, "especially since Plant Based Diets are known to cure diabetes."

A few weeks passed before we saw each other again at a car wash. I was excited because I wanted to hear his feedback. He looked uncomfortable to see me which made me a bit comfortable. There was an uneasiness in the air. With a guilty conscious he spoke. "I didn't watch the video," he admitted. "I meant to but I got so busy I couldn't find time." At first I felt sorry for him but then I understood it was on him, not me! He has to take responsibility to help himself--It's his life. I remained supportive and encouraged him to watch the cd. The sad part is he didn't even realize that the solution to his problem was right in his hands.

About two years later I ran into his sister at the mall. "How's Eric doing," I asked. "My brother's not doing well at all," she responded. "His left foot had to be amputated." I expressed my condolence with her then walked away, sad. I didn't know if it was because I knew I could help him or because he didn't have the willpower to help himself. I attended his funeral the very next year. In that moment I realized death met with ignorance is just as final as death met with intelligence. Value your life! You have the greatness within to change.

JAMMIE MORGAN BROWN

Chapter Twenty - Seven

TAKE THE PILLOW FROM YOUR HEAD AND PUT A BOOK IN IT

"A people without knowledge of self is like a tree without roots ."

Marcus Garvey

The biggest killer in the African American community is not drugs or black-on-black crime. It's Processed foods. Processed food is one of the main contributors for Heart Disease, Cancer, High Blood Pressure, Diabetes and a host of many other diseases. If you have poor health most likely what you eat has a lot to do with it.

Although getting healthy makes sense it doesn't make dollars! It appears we live in a society that has its priorities misplaced. America spends more money on healthcare than any other country in the world, yet we're sicker than most countries in the world. We are living in a new generation where our children are dying before their parents because of health related issues directly related to diet.

Unfortunately racism rears its ugly face when it's decided..who suffers most. Diabetes is a multibillion-dollar industry. People of color make up 12% of the population, yet 60% of the people on dialysis are African American.

Cancer is a multi billion-dollar business. African Americans have the highest cancer rate than any other race in the United States. African Americans are the highest recipients of high blood pressure in the entire country which generates billions. HIV/Aids, another global multibillion dollar business puts us at the top of the list.

Furthering my research I was introduced to an unfamiliar topic that really caught my attention. Question. Have you ever heard of a term used in the medical profession called, The Harvest? This is where organs and body parts are removed from your body once you die--then they're sold. The Harvest is one of the most lucrative areas in the entire medical industry. What I found to be most interesting is this.... Of all the races of people in the world, the most sought after body parts are extracted from People Of Color. This brings knew meaning to the old cliché, "Your worth more dead then alive." Are you connecting these dots!

Todays Stock Market:

Ignorance and Greed is up. Equality for all in healthcare is down. Keeping people sick is at an all time high and heavy trade!

I ATE MY WAY BACK TO HEALTH - SO CAN YOU!

Chapter Twenty - Eight

IF YOU DON'T USE IT
YOU LOOSE IT

*"I understand why children are afraid of
the dark. I don't understand why
adults are afraid of the light."*

Rashon Khan

*T*raveling to Africa and South America I couldn't help but notice the western influence on the fast food industry. Unfortunately the Caribbean is also a part of that trilogy. The indigenous loyalties to traditional foods are being gravely ignored. The reality is, the natives have abandoned the Nutritional and Healing Powers of Plants. This disturbed me because subsequently the health of the people in that region would ultimately become destabilized. As one traditional recipe is being erased another contemporary recipe is being written. The western junk food industry has hijacked the diets throughout the Diaspora leaving a good taste in pockets of American corporations. Popular chains like KFC, McDonald's, Subway, Pizza Hut and Dunkin Donuts have all become giant fixtures in this lucrative landscape. The first American fast food outlet in Kenya, KFC thrives while South Africa's appetite for fast foods makes it fertile ground for the fast food industry.

In Brazil, Bob's, originally founded in 1952 by an American entrepreneur is the second largest Brazilian fast-food hamburger chain to date.

Wendy's/Arby's international, already established in the Caribbean plans to develop a total of 24 restaurants starting with Trinidad and Tobago. The junk food industry has gone global at the expense of the people's health.

Studies prove fast foods clog the arteries causing heart problems, respiratory and cardiovascular illnesses, obesity, depression, diabetes and high blood pressure. Studies also show eating high-calorie meals with unhealthy ingredients that contain no nutritional value, poisons the body. I have another question for you. What did our elders do for food before the birth of the fast food industry? We've abandoned the herbs but the herbs haven't abandoned us. They still contain the same nutritional properties of yesterday, today.

Our communities are filled with desolate

areas. "Nature abhors a vacuum." Empty and unful-filled spaces are unnatural because they go against the laws of nature and physics.

May I ask you a question? Why can't the community revitalize desolate areas into gardens? Not only does everybody eat but now everybody eats healthy--everybody!

It's critically important to get back to nature and hold on to your traditions. It's our children's blueprint for the future. Until the lion can tell his side of the story the story will always benefit the hunter!

Chapter Twenty - Nine

KNOW THYSELF

"Lack of knowledge is darker than night."
African Proverb

I wanted to get a better understanding about the health of African American families. I read an article in a journal that said, "African Americans as a whole are sicker then any other race in America. Black men and women face the greatest risk of death from heart disease than any other race. Diabetes and obesity increases amongst African American youth." "Wow!"How did we get so sick,"I asked myself." Curious to find out I did more research. I couldn't find any medical studies to indicate precisely why African American health is on such a grave decline. This was disheartening. It pointed me back in the direction of Alternative Health Care. There I found the answer,

...you guessed it, diet!

Statistics show that social, environmental and behavioral patterns mixed with a poor diet are ingredients for a recipe called, Self Destruction, suicide! Friends and love ones dying of cancer and heart attacks or black-on-black crime has become so commonplace it no longer shocks the system. Sad but true. When it relates to health People Of Color have fallen from the pyramids to the projects.

Women Of Color are the backbones, the nurturers and the first teachers of the family. She's the mother of civilization and the Goddess of the universe. "However despite her Goddess stature they have the worst health status than any other group on nearly all the major health indices," according to Lorraine Cole President & CEO of the National Black Women's Health Project. The leading causes of death for men and women of color are heart disease, stroke, diabetes, kidney disease, HIV/Aids, lung cancer, breast cancer, colorectal cancer, pneumonia & influenza, uterine fibroids, asthma & bronchitis. As bad as it sounds here's the good news. According to many Holistic Doctor's all of these diseases/dis-eases can be reversed through proper nutrition. No matter how bad things get there's always the possibility for things to get better. The only thing that's final in life...is death.

Simple Suggestions:

1. Change-the way you look at food. Make a Promise to Yourself, to GET HEALTHY, STARTING NOW, TODAY--NOT TOMORROW!

2. Strongly consider changing to a low-fat diet first! Then gradually build from there.

3. Seek - Advice and guidance from a Licensed Nutritional Consultant, Healer, Herbalist or Licensed Wellness Center... *check references!

4. Locate Health Foods Stores in your area. Never mind The drive or expense! Your worth it and you deserve the very best!

5. Educate - Yourself about JUICING and FASTING. See food list in chapter after next.

6. EXERCISE - Has many benefits! Exercise is connected to the diet like fingers are connected to the hand. It decreases stress and tension, burns fat, builds energy, decreases depression and builds self esteem.

Consult your Physician first!
Consider Consulting with a licensed Professional Trainer.
Check References!
IMPORTANT!- DO NOT EAT ANYTHING unless you know what value it serves to your health!
And Remember...
Getting healthy is neither a sprint nor a marathon--
it's a lifestyle!

Chapter Thirty

HOW I ATE MY WAY THROUGH A BRAIN TUMOR.

"Let thy food be thy medicine let thy medicine be thy food."

Imhotep
Founder of Medicine/Ancient Egypt.

*T*he first question she asked me was, "So how did you eat your way back to health?"

"The starting point for me," I said, "was getting a clear understanding about something I read." It was the statement my Godsend had first told me a long time ago which was confirmed by both medical and holistic institutions. "Cancer cannot live in an alkaline environment." That did it for me! That was my motivation. It gave me something to aim for. The light at the end of the tunnel came into focus. I compared it to seeing the sun in the middle of a storm. Alkaline was key so I began, immediately! What does alkaline mean? It means having a pH greater than 7. PH is measured on a scale from 1 to 14. Zero to 6 relates to the acid level in the body and 7 and above, is alkaline. Let me try to simplify. Our body is made up of mostly water...correct? If the pH of that water is acidic then that is an unhealthy environment for the cells to live. If the pH of that water is alkaline then you have a healthy environment for the cells to function. Intuitively I knew that I was on the right train on the right track, heading in the right direction. I was determined to stay on that train until I heard the Conductor say...Healthy and Happy next stop!

Every morning started with two 8-ounce glasses of alkaline water, (a gallon per day). *Natural alkaline water not from a machine. 1 hour of meditation and light exercise. Mental conditioning was tough, especially at night when my mind began to drift. I had to speak it then claim it--health! Spirituality was the foundation of how I functioned. I cut off all social contact with the outside world. All negative thoughts, people, places and things was permanently banned, television included--well sort of. I did attempt to watch the Super Bowl ... as best I could.

Ahsa Ahla's Cure:

For 4 months, I juiced raw vegetables strictly.

Breakfast:

1 glass of alkaline water mixed with 3 tablespoons of Tormentilla. 1 glass of alkaline water mixed with one banana, 1-teaspoon flaxseed, 1/2 teaspoon Chia seeds and 1 teaspoon of Irish moss, 1 teaspoon of spirilina with papaya, strawberry, raspberry, or blackberries. Some mornings, I would replace juicing with a bowl of Amaranth.

Lunch:

Raw organic salads - different varieties.

Dinner:

Strictly raw green juice - Mustard Greens, Watercress, Chayote Squash, Kalaloo, Cucumber, 1/2 half of an organic green apple for 1st 5 days only.

Herbs   *formulated by Genesis 1 Nutrition.*

Cascara Sagrada, Prodigiosa, Rhubarb, Mandrake, Hydrangea, Devils claw, Senna pods, Irish Moss, Habanero 3 to 4 capsules per day with water. These herbs were used to thoroughly break up and eliminate colonic waste, cleanse the liver and kidneys, remove excess mucus from the body and revitalize the cells.

FOOD LIST

*Compiled by Ahsa Ahla *see acknowledgement.*

<u>FRUITS</u>

Apricots

Blackberry

Dates [No Medjools]

Durian

Guava

Mexican Papaya

Peaches [Yellow]

Pears

Pomegranates

Prunes

Mamey

Mango [Manilla]

Loquats

Key Limes

Yellow Grapefruits

Sour Sop [Guanabana]

Coconuts [Fresh Young not Thai]

Cherries

Oranges [Temple, Valencia]

Banana

Plums

Elderberries

Muscadines

Apples

Scuppernongs

Melons [seeded]

Noni

Watermelon [seeded]

Cherimoya

Grapes [Globe, Concords] seeded

Cactus pears {prickly pear, tuna}

Sapote

Tamarind

<u>VEGETABLES</u>

Cactus	Dulse
Okra	Irish Moss
Avocado	Kelp
Cherry Tomato	Fennel
Chayote	Scallions
Cucumbers	Spinach
Mustard Greens	Burdock
Dandelion	Cabbage
Broccoli	Kale
Mushrooms	Green Peppers
Water Crest	Pumpkin

Squash [No Yellow]

Green Beans [String Beans]

Amaranth Greens [Red Leaf Spinach]

All Sea Vegetation

GRAINS

Spelt

Quinoa

Rye

Teff

Wild Rice

Amaranth

NUTS

Almonds

Pumpkin Seeds

SWEETENERS

Coconut Palm Sugar

Maple Syrup

Vegetable Glycerin

Agave Nectar

Stevia

Chapter Thirty - One

"EACH ONE TEACH ONE"

*"The only thing that never gets tired
of running is time."*

Swahili Proverb.

Some of the greatest minds the world has ever produced suffer from poor health. These great thinkers and leaders have mastered the most complex of disciplines from politics to religion and everything else in between. Yet the most important discipline of them all still lays dormant--health & wellness, nutrition.

A friend of mine told me his seventy-year-old father had suffered two heart attacks. I asked him, "How did that happen?" With a look of uncertainty he replied, "I'm not sure because my father is always on the go! He runs nonstop but never seems to get tired. He's a very hard worker, a workaholic!"For five minutes I listened as he continued to explain--not once did he ever mention the possibility of food. I told him that hard work doesn't cause heart attacks. It's what you do when your not working hard that causes heart attacks. He looked puzzled but he continued to listen so I continued to speak. "The heart doesn't attack people," I iterated. "The function of the heart is to pump blood and deliver it throughout the body. Why would God give you a heart that would attack you?"I asked. He remained speechless. Then I said, "The reality is people attack the heart by eating foods that aren't healthy or heart friendly. You can help your father." He was quite eager and wanted to know how? I suggested that he and his father visit a health & wellness center then sit down with a nutritional consultant, for advice. The idea seemed foreign to him at first but he agreed and off they went. About a week later he called to express his sincere gratitude. He told me his father's health had improved tremendously and that he's feeling better then ever! Hearing this made me very happy. It reinforces the slogan we all should practice and preach ... Each One Teach One!

Top 10 Foods That Cause Heart Attacks.

According to National Institutes Of Health, [NIH], these

are the top 10 foods that cause heart attacks:
Fried chicken, sausages, cheesecake, steak, burgers, pizza, pasta, ice cream, doughnuts and chips. *Other statistics show that pork also, charts the list.

Helpful Tips:

*Avoid foods that are high in saturated fat, sodium and cholesterol!! Did you know every food item that you like and buy at the supermarket can be found FILLED with more nutrition at your nearest health food store? Taking care of your health should be just as important, if not more important as paying your bills.

*Pick up a cookbook on natural foods. It's perfectly okay if you don't know how to cook--it's never to late to learn -- starting now! You alone cannot save the world but on second thoughts...maybe you can. It all starts with you.

JAMIE MORGAN BROWN

Chapter Thirty - Two

"THE COST OF LIFE"

"Take care of your body today and tomorrow your body will take care of you."

Author Unknown

When you walk into a health food store one of the first things that pop out are the high food prices. It appears that eating healthy comes at a high cost. Even if you decided to eat healthier how can you afford to? A better question is how can you afford not to! Eating healthy should be the most important daily activity in your life. It dictates the quality as well as the quantity of your day--everyday!

Your body is your best friend as well as your humble servant. It wants to make you happy. It desires to please and serve you so you can accomplish your daily goals. Like the gasoline in a car your health is only as good as the food you fuel it with. Although the cost of processed food is cheaper than natural food there's still a nutritional debt to pay--your health! Processed foods are void of life, nutrient deficient. Health experts advocate that processed foods is one of the leading causes of disease. They are filled with poisons, toxins and synthetic chemicals that weaken your immune system. If the body is starving for nutrients then it can't survive. It's not the life in your food that makes you sick, it's the food in your life that makes you sick.

One of the immediate gratifications of eating healthy is feeling good--invigorated. When you feel good you're happier and the quality of your life increases. The high cost of doctor bills, gas bills and prescription drugs decreases immensely. And what about your job? No need for sick days if you're healthy, right? Time and money spent recuperating is no longer an issue. Work performance enhances, productivity increases which indicates profit--now everybody's happy. Time is money and good health is priceless!

Accept the clear fact that it's much cheaper to eat healthy so you can get healthy and stay healthy. It's your choice...the doctor bill or the food bill. It's time for me to go but don't get off until the conductor let's you know. I'll leave you with these words,

"Getting old doesn't make you sick...it's getting sick that makes you old."

Thank you and God bless.

I ATE MY WAY BACK TO HEALTH - SO CAN YOU!

Chapter Thirty - Three

"IN CLOSING"

"Write your troubles in sand but carve your blessings in stone."

Ghanian Proverb

*F*aith can move mountains so imagine what love can do. Love yourself enough to be the best you can possibly be. I hope that you will discover your greatness so that you can live the healthy life that was meant for you to live. Hopefully you have been inspired to at-least seriously think about getting healthy through nutrition. Remember, your health is your responsibility!

Embrace life and cherish every moment of it. When you close this book open your heart so you can hear Gods loving voice. May the seed of your heart smile with joy as you embrace this beautiful life that the Most High has lovingly planted. Many blessings along your journey!

JAMIE MORGAN BROWN

SURGERY PHOTOS

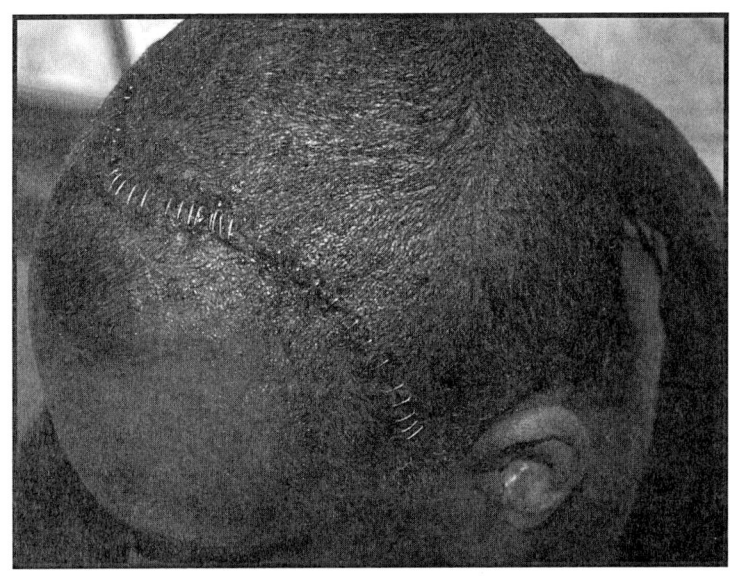

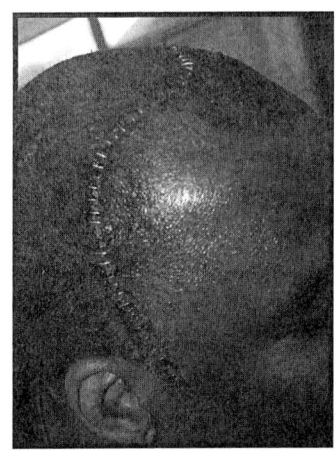

I ATE MY WAY BACK TO HEALTH - SO CAN YOU!

REFERENCES

Nutrition & Health - Ahsa Ahla

Essentials Of Nutrition And Diet Therapy
[5th edition - Sue Rodwell Williams]

INTERNET

Asthma medication

Chia seeds

5 foods to never eat

Foods that cause heart attacks

Harmful effects of dairy products

Good versus bad carbs

Lowdown on belly fat

Low carb low sugar fruits

Melanin

Nutrition facts.org

10 biggest killers of black women

10 biggest killers of black men

Why are fast foods bad?

I ATE MY WAY BACK TO HEALTH - SO CAN YOU!

ABOUT THE AUTHOR

*"Do not call the forest that
shelters you a jungle."*
Ghanian Proverb

*J*amie Morgan Brown is a writer/producer and director who hails from Jersey City, New Jersey. He is a Lifetime student of African studies at Know Thyself University. He's also a personal trainer and a master of the African martial art Capoeira Angola.

Currently, Jamie resides in Atlanta Georgia, where he's a member of the Well-Being Foundation. Their mission is building water-wells in deprived villages in Africa and throughout the diaspora. It is every human beings right to have access to clean, fresh water. Through water, life is given and the world is transformed. Even-though life isn't always tied with a bow, it's still a gift. All Life Is Precious.

JAMIE MORGAN BROWN

NOTES